Tasty Potato Recipes
Making Homemade Dishes with Potatoes

Copyright © 2021

All rights reserved.

DEDICATION

The author and publisher have provided this e-book to you for your personal use only. You may not make this e-book publicly available in any way. Copyright infringement is against the law. If you believe the copy of this e-book you are reading infringes on the author's copyright, please notify the publisher at: https://us.macmillan.com/piracy

Tasty Potato Recipes

Contents

Air Fryer Crispy Potatoes 4

Loaded Slow-Cooker Potatoes 6

Perfect Mashed Potatoes 9

Fried Mashed Potato Balls 12

Garlic Smashed Potatoes 15

German Potato Salad 18

Oven-Fried Pickle Potato Chips 21

Corned Beef Hash and Eggs 24

Instant Pot Potato Soup 27

Twice Baked Potato Casserole 30

Cheesy Potato Lasagna 33

Classic Baked Potato 36

Tasty Potato Recipes

Roasted Sweet Potato Wedges with Sweet and Spicy Yogurt Dipping Sauce 38

Rosemary Roasted Potatoes 41

Loaded Fried Mashed Potatoes 43

Twice Baked Sweet Potatoes 46

Antipasto Potato Salad 49

Bacon-Stuffed Potatoes 52

Potato Skin Burgers 55

Aloo Gobi 58

Grilled Potatoes 61

Garlic Parm Au Gratin 63

Melting Potatoes 66

Bacon-Wrapped Sweet Potato Fries 69

Tasty Potato Recipes

Air Fryer Crispy Potatoes

YIELDS: 4 SERVINGS

PREP TIME: 0 HOURS 5 MINS

TOTAL TIME: 0 HOURS 25 MINS

INGREDIENTS

Tasty Potato Recipes

1 lb. baby potatoes, halved

1 tbsp. extra-virgin olive oil

1 tsp. garlic powder

1 tsp. Italian seasoning

1 tsp. Cajun seasoning (optional)

Kosher salt

Freshly ground black pepper

Lemon wedge, for serving

Freshly chopped parsley, for garnish

DIRECTIONS

In a large bowl, toss potatoes with oil, garlic powder, Italian seasoning, and Cajun seasoning, if using. Season with salt and pepper.

Place potatoes in basket of air fryer and cook at 400° for 10 minutes. Shake basket and stir potatoes and cook until potatoes are golden and tender, 8 to 10 minutes more.

Squeeze lemon juice over cooked potatoes and garnish with parsley before serving.

Tasty Potato Recipes

Loaded Slow-Cooker Potatoes

YIELDS: 6

PREP TIME: 0 HOURS 15 MINS

COOK TIME: 5 HOURS 0 MINS

TOTAL TIME: 5 HOURS 15 MINS

Tasty Potato Recipes

INGREDIENTS

Cooking spray

2 lb. baby potatoes, halved and quartered if large

3 c. shredded Cheddar

2 cloves garlic, thinly sliced

8 slices bacon, cooked

1/4 c. sliced green onions, plus more for garnish

1 tbsp. paprika

kosher salt

Freshly ground black pepper

Sour cream, drizzling

DIRECTIONS

Line a slow cooker with foil and spray with cooking spray. Add half the potatoes, 1 1/4 cups cheese, half the garlic, 1/3 of the cooked bacon, half the green onions, and half the paprika. Season with salt and pepper. Repeat.

Tasty Potato Recipes

Cover and cook on high until potatoes are tender, 5 to 6 hours. (The bigger your potatoes, the longer they'll need.) About 20 to 30 minutes before serving, top with remaining cheese and bacon (this is your moment to make the potatoes look pretty!).

Garnish with more green onions and drizzle with sour cream before serving.

Perfect Mashed Potatoes

YIELDS: 6 - 8 SERVINGS

PREP TIME: 0 HOURS 25 MINS

TOTAL TIME: 0 HOURS 30 MINS

Tasty Potato Recipes

INGREDIENTS

3 lb. mixed potatoes, such as russets & Yukon Golds

Kosher salt

1/2 c. (1 stick) butter, plus 2 tablespoons for garnish

1/2 c. milk

1/2 c. sour cream

Freshly ground black pepper

DIRECTIONS

In a large pot, cover potatoes with water and add a generous pinch of salt. Bring to a boil and cook until totally soft, 16 to 18 minutes. Drain and return potatoes to pot.

Use a potato masher to mash potatoes until smooth.

Meanwhile, in a small saucepan, melt butter and milk until warm.

Pour over warm milk-butter mixture and stir until completely combined and creamy. Add sour cream and stir until combined.

Season mashed potatoes generously with salt and pepper.

Transfer potatoes to a serving bowl and top with remaining two tablespoons butter. Season with more pepper before serving.

Tasty Potato Recipes

Fried Mashed Potato Balls

YIELDS: 5 SERVINGS

PREP TIME: 0 HOURS 15 MINS

TOTAL TIME: 0 HOURS 25 MINS

Tasty Potato Recipes

INGREDIENTS

3 c. leftover mashed potatoes

3 slices bacon, cooked and crumbled

2/3 c. shredded cheddar cheese

2 tbsp. thinly sliced chives

1/2 tsp. garlic powder

Kosher salt

Freshly ground black pepper

2 egg, beaten

1 1/3 c. panko bread crumbs

Vegetable oil, for frying

DIRECTIONS

In a large bowl, combine mashed potatoes with cooked bacon, cheddar, chives, and garlic powder, and season with salt and pepper. Stir until all ingredients are incorporated.

Place eggs and panko in separate shallow bowls. Use a small cookie scoop to scoop 1" to 2" balls of mashed potato mixture. Roll into a ball in your hands, then dredge first in egg and then in panko. Repeat until all mashed potatoes are used.

Heat 3" of oil in a large cast iron skillet until candy thermometer reads 375°. Fry potato balls in batches until golden on all sides, 2 to 3 minutes. Drain on a paper towel lined plate and season immediately with more salt.

Tasty Potato Recipes

Garlic Smashed Potatoes

YIELDS: 4

PREP TIME: 0 HOURS 30 MINS

Tasty Potato Recipes

COOK TIME: 0 HOURS 25 MINS

TOTAL TIME: 0 HOURS 55 MINS

INGREDIENTS

1 lb. baby Yukon Gold potatoes

Kosher salt

4 tbsp. melted butter

2 cloves garlic, minced

1 tsp. fresh thyme leaves

Freshly ground black pepper

1/2 c. freshly grated Parmesan

DIRECTIONS

Preheat oven to 425°. In a large pot, cover potatoes with water and add a generous pinch of salt. Bring water to a boil and simmer until potatoes are tender, about 15 minutes. Drain and let sit until cool enough to handle.

Tasty Potato Recipes

On a large rimmed baking sheet, toss potatoes with melted butter, garlic, and thyme. Using bottom of a small glass or mason jar, press down on potatoes to smash them into flat patties.

Season with salt and pepper, then sprinkle with Parmesan.

Bake until bottoms of potatoes are beginning to crisp and Parmesan is golden, about 25 minutes.

Tasty Potato Recipes

German Potato Salad

YIELDS: 6 SERVINGS

PREP TIME: 0 HOURS 10 MINS

TOTAL TIME: 0 HOURS 40 MINS

Tasty Potato Recipes

INGREDIENTS

2 lb. baby potatoes, halved

6 slices bacon

1 red onion, finely chopped

1/4 c. apple cider vinegar

2 tbsp. water

1 tbsp. extra-virgin olive oil

1 tbsp. Dijon mustard

1/2 tsp. granulated sugar

Kosher salt

Freshly ground black pepper

8 green onions, sliced

Tasty Potato Recipes

DIRECTIONS

In a large pot, cover potatoes with water and season generously with salt. Bring water to a boil and cook until potatoes are easily pierced with a knife, 15 to 20 minutes. Drain and let cool slightly before transferring to a large serving bowl.

In a large skillet over medium heat, cook bacon until crispy, about 8 minutes. Reserve about 2 tablespoons of fat in pan, and transfer bacon to a paper towel-lined plate to drain.

Add red onion and cook over medium heat until starting to soften, about 3 minutes. Whisk in in apple cider vinegar, water, olive oil, Dijon mustard, and sugar. Bring mixture to a simmer, then turn off heat and season with salt and pepper.

Stir in green onions and gradually pour mixture over potatoes.

Toss to combine and serve warm.

Tasty Potato Recipes

Oven-Fried Pickle Potato Chips

YIELDS: 8 SERVINGS

PREP TIME: 0 HOURS 10 MINS

Tasty Potato Recipes

TOTAL TIME: 2 HOURS 0 MINS

INGREDIENTS

2 russet potatoes, thinly sliced

2 c. pickle brine

2 tbsp. olive oil

1 tbsp. freshly chopped dill, plus more for garnish

1 tsp. garlic powder

1/2 tsp. onion powder

1/2 tsp. crushed red pepper flakes (optional)

Kosher salt

Freshly ground black pepper

Ranch dressing, for dipping

Tasty Potato Recipes

DIRECTIONS

Place sliced potatoes in a large bowl and add enough pickle brine to completely submerge them. Cover with plastic wrap and refrigerate for at least 1 hour, or up to 3 hours.

Preheat oven to 400°. When potatoes are done marinating, drain and pat completely dry, then place in a large bowl. Add oil, dill, garlic powder, onion powder, and crushed red pepper flakes to bowl and toss to coat potatoes. Season with salt and pepper.

Lay potatoes in an even layer on a large baking sheet, making sure none are overlapping. Bake, flipping halfway through, until tender on the inside, and crisp and golden on the outside, about 40 minutes. Garnish with more dill and serve with ranch dressing.

Tasty Potato Recipes

Corned Beef Hash and Eggs

YIELDS: 6 SERVINGS

PREP TIME: 0 HOURS 20 MINS

Tasty Potato Recipes

TOTAL TIME: 0 HOURS 55 MINS

INGREDIENTS

3 tbsp. extra-virgin olive oil

1 onion, chopped

1 bell pepper, chopped

3 large russet potatoes, cubed

1 tsp. dried oregano

Kosher salt

Freshly ground black pepper

1 c. chopped corned beef

6 large eggs

DIRECTIONS

Preheat oven to 400°. In a large ovenproof skillet over medium heat, heat oil. Add onion and bell pepper and cook until softened, 5 minutes, then add potatoes, oregano, salt and pepper. Cook until

Tasty Potato Recipes

potatoes are golden and easily pierced with a fork, another 15 to 20 minutes. Add corned beef and cook until crispy, 5 minutes.

Make 6 wells in hash, then crack an egg into each well. Season the eggs with salt and pepper. Transfer skillet to oven and bake until whites are just set, 8 minutes.

Instant Pot Potato Soup

YIELDS: 4 SERVINGS

PREP TIME: 0 HOURS 15 MINS

TOTAL TIME: 0 HOURS 40 MINS

Tasty Potato Recipes

INGREDIENTS

2 tbsp. butter

1 large onion, chopped

2 cloves garlic, minced

1 tsp. fresh thyme leaves

6 large russet potatoes, peeled and diced

4 c. low-sodium chicken broth

1 c. plus 2 tbsp. milk, divided

2 tbsp. cornstarch

1/2 c. heavy cream

Kosher salt

Freshly ground black pepper

Shredded cheddar, for serving

Chopped cooked bacon, for serving

Freshly chopped chives, for serving

Tasty Potato Recipes

DIRECTIONS

Set Instant Pot to Sauté function and melt butter. Add onion and cook until soft, 5 minutes, then add garlic and thyme and cook until fragrant, 1 minute more.

Add potatoes and broth and place lid on Instant Pot. Set to Pressure Cook on High and set time for 8 minutes. Once finished, turn valve to quick release.

In a small bowl whisk together 2 tablespoons milk and cornstarch to make a slurry.

Remove lid from Instant Pot and set to Sauté function again. Pour in slurry, remaining 1 cup milk, and heavy cream and let boil about 5 minutes, stirring constantly. Season with salt and pepper to taste.

Garnish with cheddar, bacon, and chives before serving.

Twice Baked Potato Casserole

YIELDS: 8 SERVINGS

PREP TIME: 0 HOURS 10 MINS

TOTAL TIME: 2 HOURS 10 MINS

Tasty Potato Recipes

INGREDIENTS

6 large russet potatoes (about 3 1/2 lb.)

4 tbsp. butter, softened, plus more for pan

4 oz. cream cheese, softened

1 c. sour cream

1 1/2 c. whole milk

2 3/4 c. shredded cheddar, divided

10 slices cooked bacon, crumbled

5 green onions, sliced

3/4 tsp. garlic powder

Kosher salt

Freshly ground black pepper

DIRECTIONS

Preheat oven to 400°. Place potatoes directly on rack and bake until soft and easily pierced with the tip of a knife, 1 hour to 1 hour, 15 minutes, depending on size. Remove from oven and let cool slightly.

Tasty Potato Recipes

Slice warm potatoes in half and remove flesh with a spoon and place in a large bowl; discard skin.

Mash flesh and add butter, cream cheese, sour cream and milk and stir to combine and until butter and cream cheese is melted. Fold in 2 cups cheddar, three quarters of the bacon, three quarters of the chopped green onion, and garlic powder. Season with salt and pepper.

Brush a medium baking dish with butter and transfer potato mixture into dish. Sprinkle with remaining 3/4 cup cheddar cheese.

Bake until cheese is melty, about 20 minutes. Turn oven to broil and broil until golden, 2 to 3 minutes. Let cool 10 minutes.

Top with remaining bacon and green onions.

Cheesy Potato Lasagna

YIELDS: 8 SERVINGS

PREP TIME: 0 HOURS 25 MINS

TOTAL TIME: 1 HOUR 25 MINS

Tasty Potato Recipes

INGREDIENTS

1 tbsp. extra-virgin olive oil

1 lb. ground beef

2 cloves garlic, minced

1 tsp. Italian seasoning

Kosher salt

Freshly ground black pepper

1 (32-oz.) jar marinara

1 (16-oz.) container ricotta

1 large egg, beaten

1/2 c. freshly grated Parmesan, divided

2 tbsp. chopped basil, plus more for garnish

4 large russet potatoes, peeled and thinly sliced

2 c. shredded mozzarella

DIRECTIONS

Preheat oven to 375° and lightly grease a 9"-x-13" baking dish with

Tasty Potato Recipes

cooking spray. In a large skillet over medium heat, heat oil. Add beef, season with salt and pepper, and cook, breaking up meat with a wooden spoon, until no longer pink, about 8 minutes. Drain.

Return beef to skillet over medium heat and add garlic and Italian seasoning and cook until fragrant, 1 minute. Add marinara and let simmer until warmed through.

Combine ricotta, egg, 1/4 cup Parmesan, and basil in a large mixing bowl and season with salt and pepper. Set aside.

To prepared dish, spread a thin layer of meat sauce. Layer 1/3 of the potatoes, slightly overlapping. Spread potatoes with 1/3 of the ricotta mixture, 1/3 of the meat sauce, and 1/2 cup mozzarella. Repeat to make two more layers, then top the last layer with remaining 1 cup mozzarella and remaining 1/4 cup Parmesan.

Tent with aluminum foil and bake for 45 minutes, then remove foil and bake until cheese is golden and potatoes are fork tender, 25 minutes more.

Let rest at least 10 minutes, then garnish with basil before serving.

Classic Baked Potato

YIELDS: 4 SERVINGS

PREP TIME: 0 HOURS 5 MINS

TOTAL TIME: 1 HOUR 5 MINS

Tasty Potato Recipes

INGREDIENTS

4 russet potatoes, scrubbed

Extra-virgin olive oil

Kosher salt

Freshly ground black pepper

DIRECTIONS

Preheat oven to 350°. Pierce potatoes all over with a fork. Rub with oil and season generously with salt and pepper, then place on a baking sheet.

Bake until potatoes are easily pierced with a fork, 1 hour to 1 hour 30 minutes.

Tasty Potato Recipes

Roasted Sweet Potato Wedges with Sweet and Spicy Yogurt Dipping Sauce

YIELDS: 4 SERVINGS

PREP TIME: 0 HOURS 10 MINS

Tasty Potato Recipes

TOTAL TIME: 0 HOURS 30 MINS

INGREDIENTS

3 large sweet potatoes (about 1 1/2 lbs.), cut into 1/2" wedges

2 tbsp. extra-virgin olive oil

1 tsp. paprika

1/2 tsp. ground cumin

Kosher salt

Freshly ground black pepper

1 TWO GOOD Vanilla Greek Lowfat Yogurt (5.3-oz. Container)

1/2 large jalapeño, minced

1 tsp. lime zest, plus more for garnish

1 tbsp. lime juice

DIRECTIONS

Preheat oven to 425°. On a rimmed baking sheet, toss sweet potatoes

Tasty Potato Recipes

with oil, paprika, and cumin. Season with salt and pepper and spread into a single layer. Roast until golden, turning ½ way through, about 25 minutes.

In a small bowl, combine yogurt with jalapeño, lime zest, and juice. Season with salt and pepper.

Serve warm potato wedges with sauce and more lime zest over top.

Rosemary Roasted Potatoes

YIELDS: 6

PREP TIME: 0 HOURS 10 MINS

TOTAL TIME: 1 HOUR 10 MINS

Tasty Potato Recipes

INGREDIENTS

2 lb. baby potatoes, halved or quartered if large

2 tbsp. extra-virgin olive oil

4 cloves garlic, minced

2 tbsp. freshly chopped rosemary

kosher salt

Freshly ground black pepper

Fresh rosemary sprigs, for serving

DIRECTIONS

Preheat oven to 400°. Add potatoes to baking sheet. Toss with olive oil, garlic, and rosemary and season generously with salt and pepper.

Roast until crispy, stirring occasionally, 1 hour to 1 hour 15 minutes.

Add more rosemary sprigs for serving.

Loaded Fried Mashed Potatoes

YIELDS: 4

PREP TIME: 0 HOURS 20 MINS

Tasty Potato Recipes

TOTAL TIME: 0 HOURS 20 MINS

INGREDIENTS

Vegetable oil, for frying

2 1/2 c. mashed potatoes

1/2 c. shredded cheddar

1 large egg, beaten

1 tbsp. finely chopped chives, plus more for garnish

1/2 tsp. hot sauce

1/2 tsp. kosher salt

All-purpose flour (optional)

1 Sour cream, for serving

DIRECTIONS

In a large skillet over medium heat, add enough oil to fill pan a third of the way up. In a large bowl, stir potatoes, cheese, egg, chives, hot sauce, and salt until combined. (If your mashed potatoes are a little runny, add flour one tablespoon at a time until you can form dough balls.)

Working in batches, scoop heaping tablespoons of mixture and drop into hot oil. Fry until golden on both sides, about 2 minutes per side.

Top potatoes with sour cream and chives before serving.

Tasty Potato Recipes

Twice Baked Sweet Potatoes

YIELDS: 6 SERVINGS

PREP TIME: 0 HOURS 20 MINS

TOTAL TIME: 1 HOUR 35 MINS

Tasty Potato Recipes

INGREDIENTS

6 large sweet potatoes, scrubbed clean

1 tbsp. extra-virgin olive oil

Kosher salt

1/2 c. milk

1/4 c. sour cream

4 tbsp. melted butter

1 1/2 c. shredded Monterey Jack, divided

1 c. black beans, rinsed and drained

2 green onions, thinly sliced, plus more for garnish

2 cloves garlic, minced

1 c. quartered grape tomatoes

1 avocado, cubed

1 small jalapeño, sliced into rounds

1/4 c. crumbled queso fresco

Tasty Potato Recipes

DIRECTIONS

Preheat oven to 375°. Pat potatoes completely dry with paper towels. Poke potatoes all over with a fork, then rub with oil and sprinkle with salt. Place directly on oven racks and bake until pierced easily with a fork, about 1 hour. Place on a large baking sheet and let cool until cool enough to handle.

Cut a thin layer off the top of each potato lengthwise. Scoop out insides of each potato, leaving a ½" border. Place insides in large bowl. (You can keep the potato tops and roast them on the tray as a snack!)

Into the bowl with the potatoes, add milk, sour cream, and butter. Mash until all ingredients are incorporated and mixture is mostly smooth. Fold in 1 cup Monterey Jack, black beans, green onions, and garlic and season with salt.

Fill baked potatoes with mixture and place on a large baking sheet. Top with remaining ½ cup of Monterey Jack. Bake until cheese is melty and outside is crispy, 15 minutes.

Top with tomatoes, avocado, jalapeño, and queso fresco before serving.

Tasty Potato Recipes

Antipasto Potato Salad

YIELDS: 6 SERVINGS

PREP TIME: 0 HOURS 15 MINS

TOTAL TIME: 0 HOURS 25 MINS

Tasty Potato Recipes

INGREDIENTS

2 lb. red skinned baby potatoes, halved

4 oz. thinly sliced salami, chopped

4 oz. provolone cheese, cut into 1/2" cubes

1/2 c. diced red bell pepper

1/2 c. diced green bell pepper

1/2 c. artichoke hearts, drained and chopped

1/2 c. black olives, sliced

1/2 small red onion, finelly chopped

1/4 c. extra-virgin olive oil

2 tbsp. red wine vinegar

Large pinch red pepper flakes

Basil leaves, for garnish

Tasty Potato Recipes

DIRECTIONS

In a large pot, cover potatoes with water and season generously with salt. Bring water to a boil and cook until potatoes are easily pierced with a knife, 8 to 10 minutes. Drain and let cool slightly before transferring to a large serving bowl.

In a medium bowl, whisk the olive oil with the red wine vinegar. Add red pepper flakes and season with salt and pepper.

In a large bowl, combine the salami, provolone, bell peppers, artichoke, olives, and red onion with the potatoes.

Pour the dressing over the potato mixture and gently toss to combine. Serve with basil leaves.

Tasty Potato Recipes

Bacon-Stuffed Potatoes

YIELDS: 4 SERVINGS

PREP TIME: 0 HOURS 15 MINS

TOTAL TIME: 1 HOUR 0 MINS

Tasty Potato Recipes

INGREDIENTS

4 large yukon gold (or small russets), scrubbed clean

2 tbsp. extra-virgin olive oil

2 tbsp. melted butter

2 tsp. garlic powder

1 tsp. dried oregano

1/2 tsp. paprika

Kosher salt

Freshly ground black pepper

6 slices bacon, cut into 2" pieces

1 c. shredded mozzarella

1/4 c. grated Parmesan

DIRECTIONS

Preheat oven to 425°. Make small slits in each potato, like an accordion, making sure not to cut all the way through. Place potatoes on a small sheet pan.

Tasty Potato Recipes

In a small bowl, whisk together oil, melted butter, oregano, and paprika and season with salt and pepper. Brush all over potatoes.

Insert a piece of bacon into each slit, then sprinkle potatoes with mozzarella and Parmesan. Bake until potatoes are tender and bacon is crispy, about 45 minutes, brushing with remaining butter mixture halfway through if desired.

Garnish with chives before serving.

Tasty Potato Recipes

Potato Skin Burgers

YIELDS: 4

PREP TIME: 0 HOURS 20 MINS

TOTAL TIME: 2 HOURS 10 MINS

Tasty Potato Recipes

INGREDIENTS

4 Yukon gold potatoes

kosher salt

Freshly ground black pepper

2 tbsp. extra-virgin olive oil

1 lb. ground beef

6 slices bacon, cooked and crumbled

1 1/2 c. shredded Cheddar

1/2 c. sour cream

1 tbsp. chopped fresh chives

DIRECTIONS

Preheat oven to 350°. Season potatoes with salt and pepper and rub with olive oil. Bake until tender, 1 hour 30 minutes. Raise oven temperature to 450°.

Let potatoes cool, then halve lengthwise and scoop out potatoes, leaving 1/4" potato on all sides.

Tasty Potato Recipes

Place potato skins facedown and brush with oil. Bake until golden, 10 minutes.

Meanwhile, shape ground beef into burgers the same size as buns. Season with salt and pepper and cook until medium, 5 minutes per side.

Flip and fill potato skins with bacon and cheese. Return to oven until cheese is melty, 5 minutes.

Fill skins with sour cream and chives, then top one with a cooked burger and another potato skin.

Serve.

Tasty Potato Recipes

Aloo Gobi

YIELDS: 6 SERVINGS

PREP TIME: 0 HOURS 15 MINS

TOTAL TIME: 0 HOURS 40 MINS

Tasty Potato Recipes

INGREDIENTS

2 tbsp. vegetable oil

1 red chili, diced

2 cloves garlic, minced

1 tbsp. minced ginger

1 tsp. garam masala

1/2 tsp. dried turmeric

1/4 tsp. cayenne pepper

3 russets, peeled and chopped into 1" pieces

1 medium head cauliflower, cut into florets

1 c. low-sodium vegetable broth

Kosher salt

Freshly ground black pepper

Freshly chopped cilantro, for serving

Tasty Potato Recipes

DIRECTIONS

In a large skillet over medium-high heat, heat oil. Add chili, garlic, and ginger and cook until fragrant, 1 minute. Add garam masala, turmeric, and cayenne and cook until toasted, 1 minute more.

Add potatoes, cauliflower, and vegetable broth and season with salt and pepper. Reduce heat and cook, covered, until potatoes and cauliflower are tender, 15 minutes. Garnish with cilantro to serve.

Grilled Potatoes

YIELDS: 4 - 6 SERVINGS

PREP TIME: 0 HOURS 5 MINS

TOTAL TIME: 0 HOURS 20 MINS

Tasty Potato Recipes

INGREDIENTS

4 large Idaho or russet potatoes, cut into wedges

2 tsp. garlic powder

1 tsp. kosher salt

1 tsp. freshly ground black pepper

1/2 c. extra-virgin olive oil

2 tbsp. freshly chopped herbs (such as parsley)

DIRECTIONS

Bring a well-salted pot of water to a boil, then add potatoes and cook until al dente, 5 to 7 minutes. Drain and let cool slightly.

Heat grill to medium-high and oil grates. In a large bowl, mix together garlic powder, salt, and pepper, then stir in olive oil. Add potatoes and toss gently to coat. Remove potatoes from oil and reserve excess in oil in bowl.

Grill potatoes, flipping once, until golden brown, about 5 minutes.

Add herbs to reserved oil mixture, then return potatoes to mixture and toss again.

Tasty Potato Recipes

Garlic Parm Au Gratin

YIELDS: 6

PREP TIME: 0 HOURS 15 MINS

TOTAL TIME: 1 HOUR 30 MINS

Tasty Potato Recipes

INGREDIENTS

Butter, for pan

3 lb. russet potatoes

2 1/2 c. half-and-half

3 cloves garlic, minced

1 tsp. chopped thyme leaves

2 c. freshly grated Parmesan, divided

kosher salt

Freshly ground black pepper

DIRECTIONS

Preheat oven to 375°. Grease a large baking dish all over with butter and place on top of a baking sheet (to catch any cream that might overflow). Peel potatoes then cut into very thin slices, about ¼" thick. (Using a mandoline if you have one!) Place in a bowl and cover with water to prevent browning.

In a small saucepan over medium heat, combine half-and-half, garlic and thyme. Heat mixture until bubbles begin to form around the

Tasty Potato Recipes

edges. Stir in 1 ½ cups Parmesan then season with salt and pepper. Remove from heat.

Drain potatoes and pat dry with paper towels or a clean kitchen towel. Arrange potatoes in the baking dish, fanning the potatoes to look like shingles. Pour warm cream mixture over the potatoes and press down on the potatoes to make sure that every potato is coated. Sprinkle with remaining Parmesan.

Bake until the top is bubbling and golden and the potatoes are tender, about 1 hour 15 minutes.

Serve warm.

Melting Potatoes

YIELDS: 4

COOK TIME: 0 HOURS 45 MINS

TOTAL TIME: 0 HOURS 50 MINS

Tasty Potato Recipes

INGREDIENTS

2 lb. Yukon Gold potatoes, peeled

2 tbsp. butter, melted

2 tbsp. olive oil

2 tbsp. chopped fresh rosemary

3/4 tsp. salt

1/4 tsp. Pepper

1 c. low-sodium chicken broth

2 garlic cloves, finely minced

DIRECTIONS

Preheat oven to 500 degrees F.

Cut potatoes into ¾"-1" thick slices, and place the slices in a medium bowl. Pour in the olive oil, melted butter and rosemary. Season with salt and pepper and toss until evenly combined.

Lay the potatoes flat, in a single layer, on a 9"x13" metal baking dish, using two dishes if necessary. (Do not use a glass baking dish, as pouring the chicken broth into the hot pan could resulting in the glass cracking.) Bake until the bottom of each potato is golden brown, about 15 minutes.

Remove the dish from the oven and flip each potato. Bake for another 15 minutes, until the other side of the potato is golden brown.

Remove dish from oven, pour in chicken broth and sprinkle with garlic. Return to oven to bake until the potatoes are tender and the stock reduces slightly, about another 15 minutes.

Serve warm with extra sauce drizzled on top.

Bacon-Wrapped Sweet Potato Fries

YIELDS: 1

PREP TIME: 0 HOURS 10 MINS

TOTAL TIME: 0 HOURS 45 MINS

Tasty Potato Recipes

INGREDIENTS

3 large sweet potatoes, cut into fries

18 slices bacon

2 tsp. chili powder

Freshly ground black pepper

BBQ sauce, for serving

Ranch, for serving

DIRECTIONS

Preheat oven to 400° and set a rack over a baking sheet (to catch the bacon grease). Wrap each fry with one slice bacon and season with chili powder and pepper.

Bake until sweet potatoes are tender and bacon is crispy, 33 to 35 minutes.

Serve with BBQ sauce and/or ranch.

Printed in Great Britain
by Amazon